ELGAR

Great is the Lord

PSALM 48 • OPUS 67

Anthem for SATB & organ or orchestra

Order No: NOV 070461R

NOVELLO PUBLISHING LIMITED
8/9 Frith Street, London W1V 5TZ

To the Very Reverend J. Armitage Robinson, D.D., Dean of Wells.

With sincere regard.

An anthem for the foundation or commemoration of a church,
or for general use.

First performed in Westminster Abbey, 16 July 1912

FULL SCORE AND ORCHESTRAL MATERIAL ON HIRE

No part of this publication may be copied or reproduced in any form or by any means without the prior permission of Novello & Company Limited.

Permission to perform this work in public must be obtained from The Performing Right Society Limited, 29/33 Berners Street, London W1P 4AA or from the affiliated Society overseas.

GREAT IS THE LORD.

Psalm xlviii.

EDWARD ELGAR (Op. 67).

Copyright, 1912, by Novello and Company, Limited.
Copyright renewed 1940.

1st Sopranos.
A
Animato.
beau - ti-ful in e - le -
2nd Sopranos.
beau - ti-ful in e - le -
1st & 2nd Altos.
Allargando.
ho - - - - - - li - ness; . .
beau - ti-ful in e - le -
Tenors. Allargando.
ho - - - - - - li - ness; . .
Basses. Allargando.
ho - - - - - - li - ness; . .
Animato.
A
Sw.
Allargando.
- va - tion,— the joy of the whole earth,— is mount Zi - - - -
- va - tion,— the joy . . of the whole earth,— is mount Zi - on, . . .
- va - tion,— the joy . . of the whole earth,— is mount Zi - on, . . .

B
on, on the sides . . . . of the north, ...
on the sides . . . . of the north, ...
on the sides . . . . of the north, ...
B
f Gt. (Sw. coupled.)
f
1st & 2nd Sopranos.
f
beau - - ti - ful in e - - le -
Altos.
f
great is the Lord . . . and great - ly to be
Tenors.
f
great is the Lord . . . and great - ly to be
Basses.
f
great is the Lord . . . and great - ly to be
Gt.

- va - tion,— the joy of the whole earth,— is mount Zi - on, mount
prais - - - - - ed . . . . . in the ci - ty of our
prais - - - - - ed . . . . . in the ci - ty of our
prais - - - - - ed . . . . . in the ci - ty of our
Zi - on, on the sides.. of the north, .. the ci - ty, the
God, in the moun - tain of His ho - - - - - li - ness. . .
God, in the moun - tain of His ho - - - - - li - ness. . .
God, in the moun - tain of His ho - - - - - li - ness. . .

C

f

ci - ty of the great King. . . God hath made Himself

dim. *f*

. . . . God hath made Himself

dim. *f*

. . . . God hath made Himself

dim. *f*

. . . . God hath made Himself

C *Gt.*

dim. L.H. *f* 8 *ft.*

known in her pal - a - ces for a re - - - - - fuge, for a

p

known in her pal - a - ces for a re - - - - - fuge.

dim.

known in her pal - a - ces for a re - - - - - fuge.

dim.

known in her pal - a - ces for a re - - - - - fuge.

R.H.

sf *dolce.* *p*

f *p*

re - - - fuge. . . . . . . ,
dim.
Sw.
rit.
pp
dim.
pp
D
Allegro moderato.
mf ma molto marcato.
cres.
For, lo! the kings as-sem-bled themselves, they pass-ed by to -
mf ma molto marcato.
cres.
For, lo! the kings as-sem-bled themselves, they pass-ed by to -
mf ma molto marcato.
cres.
For, lo! the kings as-sem-bled themselves, they pass-ed by to -
mf ma molto marcato.
cres.
For, lo! the kings as-sem-bled themselves, they pass-ed by to -
D
Allegro moderato. = of preceding movement.
Full Sw. (closed.) molto marcato.
sempre staccato.
cres.
f 8, 16, 32. staccato.

- ge - ther; . . . they saw, then were they a - maz - ed;
- ge - ther; . . . they saw, then were they a - maz - ed;
- ge - ther; . . . they saw, then were they a - maz - ed;
- ge - ther; . . . they saw, then were they a - maz - ed;
Gt.
più sostenuto.
they were dis - may'd, ... they hast-ed a -
they were dis - may'd, ... they hast-ed a -
they were dis - may'd, ... they hast-ed a -
they were dis - may'd, ... they hast-ed a -
dim.
ten.
ten.
ten.

- way, they hasted a - way;

- way, they hasted a - way; trembling took hold of them

- way, they hast-ed a-way; trembling took hold of them

- way, they hast-ed a-way; trem -

Sw.

mp

Sw.

p

pp

E

1st Sopranos.

pain, . . . as of a wo-man in tra - vail,— . .

there,— . . . .

there,— . . . .

- - bling took hold of them there,—

E

p Ch.

Sw.

1st Sopranos.
2nd Sopranos. cres. molto.
pain, . . . as of a wo-man in tra - vail,— . . as with the
Altos.
as with the
Tenors.
as with the
Basses.
as with the
Gt. staccato.
mf
cres.
cres. molto.
Sw.
p
Reeds. ff
cres.
east wind that break - - - - - - - eth the ships of
ff
Gt.
Tuba.
dim.

1st & 2nd Sopranos.
dim.
Tar - - - shish, . . that breaketh the ships . . . of
Altos.
dim.
Tar - - - shish, . . that breaketh the ships . . . of
Tenors.
dim.
Tar - - - shish, . . that breaketh the ships . . . of
Basses.
dim.
Tar - - - shish, . . that breaketh the ships . . . of
Sw.
dim.
F
p cres.
sempre cres.
Tar - shish: lo! the kings as - sem-bled themselves, they
p cres.
sempre cres.
Tar - shish: lo! the kings as - sem-bled themselves, they
p cres.
sempre cres.
Tar - shish: lo! the kings as - sem-bled themselves, they
p cres.
sempre cres.
Tar - shish: lo! the kings as - sem-bled themselves, they
F
sf
pp
cres.
dim.

pass - ed by . . to - ge - ther ; they saw, . . then were they a - maz - ed,
pass - ed by . . to - ge - ther ; they saw, . . then were they a - maz - ed, they were dis -
pass - ed by . . to - ge - ther ; they saw, . . then were they a - maz - ed ; they were dis -
pass - ed by . . to - ge - ther ; they saw, . . then were they a - maz - ed, they were dis -
sempre cres.
più sostenuto.
Poco allargando.
they were a - maz - ed ; . . . .
- may'd, . . . they were a - maz - ed ; they were dis -
- may'd, . . . they were a - maz - ed ; . . . .
- may'd, . . . they were a - maz - ed ; they were dis -
Poco allargando.

a tempo.
. . they were dis - may'd, they were dis - may'd, they hast-ed a -
a tempo.
- may'd, they were dis - may'd, they were dis - may'd, they hast-ed a -
a tempo.
. . they were dis - may'd, they were dis - may'd, they hast-ed a -
a tempo.
- may'd, they were dis - may'd, they were dis - may'd, they hast-ed a -
a tempo.
dim.
sonoramente.
dim.
- way, they hast-ed a - way, they hast-ed a - way.
dim.
- way, they hast-ed a - way, they hast-ed a - way.
dim.
- way, they hast ed a - way, they hast-ed a - way.
dim.
- way, they hast-ed a - way, they hast-ed a - way.
Sw.
p
Ch.

G
Recit. Maestoso.
As we have heard, so have we seen in the city of the Lord of
so have we seen in the city of the Lord of
f Gt. 8 ft.
f 16, 32.
Quasi Recit. maestoso.
solenne.
hosts, in the city of the Lord of hosts, in the city of our God: God will es-
hosts, in the city of the Lord of hosts, in the city of our God: . .
Sw.
pp cres.
pp 16.

1st Sopranos.
ff Lento.
-tab-lish it for ev - er, for ev - er.
2nd Sopranos.
ff
-tab-lish it for . . ev - er, for ev - er.
Altos.
f
ff
for ev - er, for ev - er.
Tenors.
f
ff
for . . ev - er, for ev - er.
Basses.
f
ff
for . . ev - er, for ev - er.
Lento.
Gt.
rit.
p
dim.
H
Andante. Bass Solo.
p
We have thought on Thy lov-ing-kind-ness, O God, in the
H
Andante.
Sw. (or Ch.)
p
pp
pp
p Ch.
p
Ch. coupled.
p
midst of Thy tem - - ple: . . as is Thy name. O
cres.

God, so is Thy praise un-to the ends . . of the earth, un-to the
16. p

molto espress.
rit.
Poco più mosso
ends . . . of the earth; Thy right hand is full of
Poco più mosso.
rit.
colla parte.

f
right - - - - - - eous-ness, . . . Thy right hand is
mp (Gt.)

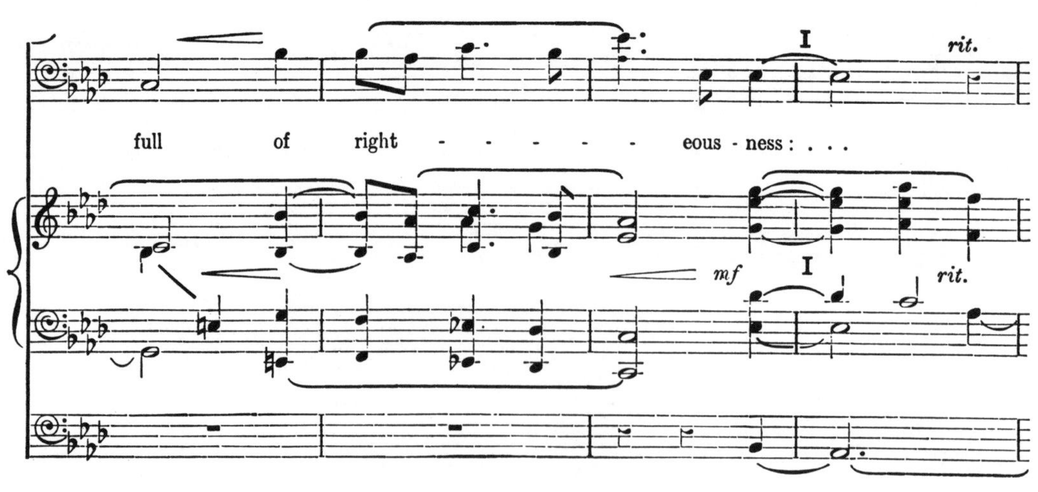
I
rit.
full of right - - - - - - eous - ness : . . .
mf
I
rit.

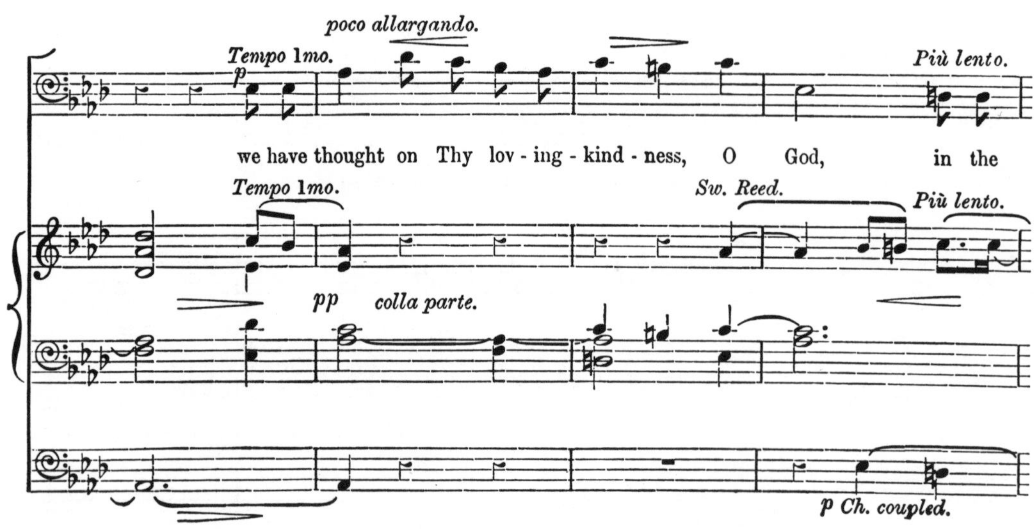
poco allargando.
Tempo 1mo.
p
Più lento.
we have thought on Thy lov - ing - kind - ness, O God, in the
Tempo 1mo.
Sw. Reed.
Più lento.
pp
colla parte.
p Ch. coupled.

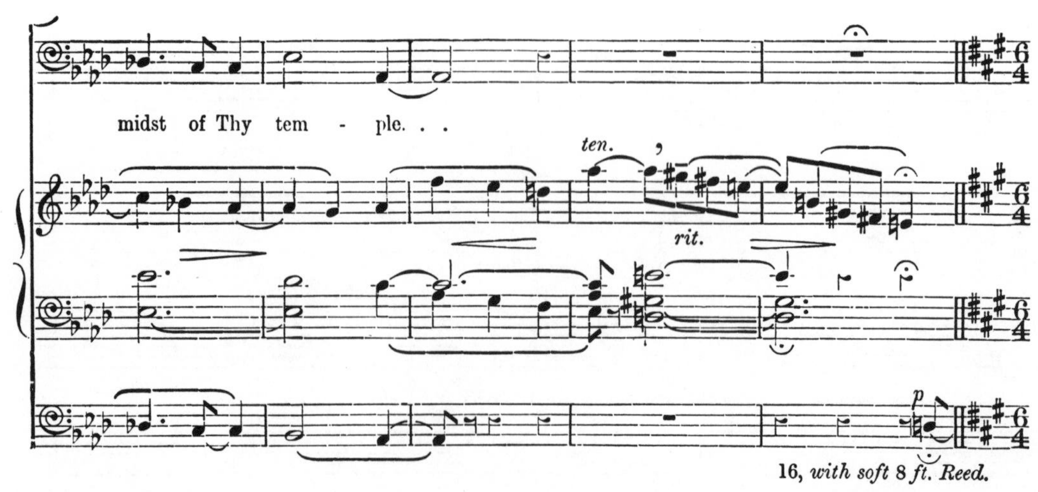
midst of Thy tem - ple. . .
ten.
rit.
p
16, with soft 8 ft. Reed.

J
Andantino.
p
Let mount Zi - on be glad,
let mount Zi - on be
Let mount Zi - on be glad,
let mount Zi - on be
Let mount Zi - on be glad,
Let mount Zi - on be glad,
J
Andantino.
p
glad,
let the daugh - ters of Ju - - dah re -
glad,
let the daugh - ters of Ju - - dah re -
let mount Zi - on be glad, . . . glad, be - cause of Thy
let mount Zi - on be glad, . . . glad, be - cause of Thy

- joice,

- joice, let the daugh - ters of Ju - - dah re - joice,

judge - ments, let the daugh - ters of

judge - - ments, glad, be- cause of Thy judge - - ments, . .

let mount Zi - on be glad, let mount Zi - on be

let mount Zi - on be glad, let mount Zi - on be

Ju - - dah re - joice, let mount Zi - on be glad,

. . let mount Zi - on be glad,

glad, . . . be glad, be-cause of Thy judge - ments;

glad,

let the daugh-ters of Ju - - dah re-joice;

let mount Zi - on be glad, let the daugh-ters of

cres.

walk a-bout Zi - - on . . and

glad, be cause of Thy judge - - ments;

cres.

walk a-bout Zi - - on . . and

Ju - - dah re - joice; . . .

cres.

K ($\text{half} = \text{dotted half}$)

go round a - bout her,

walk a - bout Zi - - on,

go round a - bout her,

walk a - bout Zi - - on, *f* tell the

K

cres.

Gt. *f*

f 16.

f con - sid - er her

f con - sid - er her

f mark ye well her bul - warks, con - sid - er her

towers there-of, ... *f* con - sid - er her

f Gt.

pal - a - ces, that ye may tell it to the gen - - - - er -
pal - a - ces, that ye may
pal - a - ces, that ye may
pal - a - ces, that ye may
Gt. (Sw. coupled). f
- a - - tion fol - low - ing. For
tell it to the gen - er - a - tion fol - low - ing. For
tell it to the gen - er - a - tion fol - low - ing. For
tell it to the gen - er - a - tion fol - low - ing. For
Gt.
32.

Moderato (come prima) più maestoso.

ff

this God is our God for ev - er and ev - - - - -

this God is our God for ev - er and ev - - - - -

this God is our God for ev - er and ev - - - - -

this God is our God for ev - er and ev - - - - -

Moderato (come prima) più maestoso.

ff

- - - - - - - - - er, for this God is our God for

- - - - - - - - - er, for this God is . . our God for . .

- - - - - - - - - er, for this God is . . our God for . .

- - - - - - - er, for this God is . . our God for . .

legato.

sempre legato.

ev - er and ev - - - - - - - - - er; . . .
ev - er and ev - - - - - - - - - er; . . .
ev - er and ev - - - - - - - - - er; . . . He . . .
ev - er and ev - - - - - - - - - er; . . . He . . .
1st Sopranos.
M
He . . . . will be our guide:
2nd Sopranos.
He . . .
Altos.
He . . .
Tenors.
. . . will be our guide, He will be our guide:
Basses.
. . . will be our guide, He will be our guide:
M

for this God is our . . God; He will be our
. . will be our guide e-ven un-to death:
. . will be our guide e-ven un-to death, He will be our
for this God is . . our God for
for this God is . . our God for
ff
rit.
sf
guide: . . for this God . . . . . is . .
for this God is . . our God, ... is . .
guide e-ven . . un - - to death, e-ven un - - to
ev - - - - - - - - - - - - - er and ev - - er; . .
ev - - - - - - - - - - - - - - er and ev - - er; . .

1st & 2nd SOPRANOS. Tranquillo.
N
p
our God; . . . . He will be our guide . . . .
ALTOS.
p
death, He . . . . . . will be our guide . . . .
TENORS.
p
. . He . . . . . . will be our guide . . . .
BASSES.
p
. . He will be our guide . . . .
N
Tranquillo.
Sw.
p
Ch. legato.
p
legato.
. . e - ven . . un - to death, ... un - to
. . e - ven . . un - to death, ... un - to
. . e - ven . . un - to death, ... un - to
. . e - ven . . un - to death, ... un - to

Printed and bound in Great Britain by
Caligraving Limited Thetford Norfolk

1/01 (39278)